Paralegal's Guide to Credit Repair

by

Robin Bull

I0476668

Black Moth Publications

PARALEGAL'S GUIDE TO CREDIT REPAIR

PARALEGAL'S GUIDE TO CREDIT REPAIR

and identifying details have been changed to protect the privacy of individuals.

Disclaimer: This book is NOT meant to act as legal advice. This book is for informational purposes only. If you have legal questions about debt or credit, please consult a qualified and licensed attorney in your area. This is information that is found on the Internet in various places (including the FTC's consumer website that covers the FDCPA). It is also a summary of what I've learned during my experience as a bankruptcy paralegal.

PARALEGAL'S GUIDE TO CREDIT REPAIR

Introduction

I've got a secret for you. It's one that you're probably not going to like. Yet, I urge you to read it (and the rest of this book). In reality, what I'm about to tell you is, ultimately, good news. There is no magic secret to fixing your credit. When you see signs that advertise how your credit can be "repaired" for a one-time payment or monthly payments, you're not getting anything that you really couldn't do for yourself. If you don't believe me, check out the FTC's consumer website about credit repair. It'll tell you what I just told you.

That's good news, though. It means that you can save yourself hundreds of dollars (in some instances) per month. It means all you have to do is read this book (and use the example letters included or write your own).

So, then, why do people charge for credit repair and is it legal? First, yes…it's legal. Now, the kicker here is that if you elect to go ahead and pay someone to do this for you, you should

PARALEGAL'S GUIDE TO CREDIT REPAIR

check their references and their experience. You need to make sure that the person or organization that you're paying can get the job done for you. So, why do people pay to have it done? Because this sort of work is a convenience service. It's a bit like hiring a personal cook. Sure, you could cook for yourself, but some people don't have the time or the inclination to do it. They pay someone to do it for them. It's the same concept for people who hire a maid. Credit repair is a convenience service. If, after you read this book, you decide that you still want to pay someone to do this for you, that's okay. You're allowed to do that. Some people don't have the time or they just don't want to do this on their own. Just take the service for what it is – a convenience.

Alright, so who am I to tell you that there's no big secret and that you can do this on your own? My name is Robin Bull. I have a Bachelor's in Paralegal Studies (Summa Cum Laude). More importantly, I am a former bankruptcy analyst and senior paralegal for a bankruptcy company. What's a bankruptcy company? It's a company that contacts corporations and offers to file claims against bankruptcy estates on their behalf in the hopes that there are assets. My job as a bankruptcy analyst and paralegal was twofold. I filed claims and I worked with the United States Trustees to ensure that they got the documentation that they needed from those corporations that hired us. This gave me an inside glimpse of what is required to prove that a debt is truly owed. It also

PARALEGAL'S GUIDE TO CREDIT REPAIR

opened my eyes to the fact that many debt buyers cannot prove (to the Trustee's satisfaction) that the debt should be paid.

That's why I wrote this book. You can fix your own credit. You can use what I know about debt collectors to do it. In this book, we'll discuss how you can get your credit reports, how you should list your debts, and the options that you have to dispute it…because that's really all you're doing (unless you've truly been a victim of identity theft). I'll give you some ideas on how you can challenge the debt, letter templates that you can send, and what you should do if you really owe the debt.

1

What You Need to Know About Credit

Everyone has a general understanding of credit. It's when you get a good or a service first and pay for it later. If you make car payments, that's credit. If you pay an electricity bill, that's credit. If you have a credit card, that's credit. Your credit affects more than just your ability to get the things that you want and need. Your credit also affects your ability to get a job and the rates that you pay for car insurance.

Another concept related to credit is your credit score. The higher the number, the better your credit. This means that you make payments on time or pay things off when you should. This is a big determining factor for many major purchases in life.

Good credit means that you get good interest rates. It means that you are less of a credit risk. It means that you have a decent debt-to-income ratio (meaning that you haven't taken out more than you can reasonably pay off).

PARALEGAL'S GUIDE TO CREDIT REPAIR

People who have bad credit aren't awful. It can happen to anyone at any time. For many of us, it just takes one major medical catastrophe or a job loss to send us into the land of bad credit.

There are three options if you have bad credit. You can look at filing bankruptcy. Bankruptcy affects your credit for years. You can only file every so many years (depending on the chapter). You have to meet a certain income requirement. It can be expensive. You can simply begin to pay off your past-due debt. If you choose this option, you really have to stay on top of contacting those creditors to ensure that they update your credit report. We will talk about settling debt in a later chapter. If you plan to settle your debt, please skip to that chapter now and read it. Finally, there's credit repair…which is the reason why you bought this book.

What Is Credit Repair and How Does It Work?

Credit repair is a methodical set of steps that you can take to remove inaccuracies from your credit report. When I say inaccuracies I mean things that you've paid off (always keep zero balance statements), things that aren't yours (potential identity theft or if you're a junior or senior you may notice a bleed over from your namesake's credit), or things that are legally too old to be on your credit report.

PARALEGAL'S GUIDE TO CREDIT REPAIR

The basics in how it works, that we will discuss in detail, is simple. You request all three of your credit reports. You do not need your credit score. You examine your reports. Make a list of each (and we will talk about why very soon). Then, begin to contact the bureaus or the debtors to dispute the information. The credit bureaus give a certain amount of time for the creditor to respond with proof. If they don't respond, it is removed from your credit.

See? I told you there was no secret. Now, something you should keep in mind is that when you're dealing with debt collectors, as you may have to do in addition to contacting the credit bureaus), you must be careful not to say or do something that would allow them to believe that you're taking responsibility for the debt. In some instances, this can renew the statute of limitations on collections (which we will talk about later). I am not an attorney and I cannot give you specific information on whether something will or will not renew the right to collect. The only person that can give you that sort of information is a licensed attorney in good standing with the bar. The information that you're getting from me is public information.

As the inaccurate information is either collected or removed, you'll begin to see your credit score improve. For your credit score to continue to go up, it's important that you keep up with all of your monthly payments. You should pay on time or

PARALEGAL'S GUIDE TO CREDIT REPAIR

early.

Getting a Free Copy of Your Credit Report

I mentioned a little earlier in this chapter that you need to get your credit report. You are entitled to a free copy of your credit report each year. I mean totally free – you don't have to sign up for a credit monitoring service. You don't have to sign up for credit score monitoring. Nothing. You need to get a copy from all three major credit bureaus. Luckily, there is a website set up to do just that. You go through the steps and answer the security questions. Then, you can download each one in PDF format. Once you have them, you can print them out. It will make comparing them easier which we will talk about in the next chapter. To get your free credit reports go to: www.annualcreditreport.com.

PARALEGAL'S GUIDE TO CREDIT REPAIR

2

Your Debts

Now that you have your credit reports, you're ready to get started. First, you want to compare all of your credit reports. They should all have essentially the same debts. So, what are you looking for?

o Look for duplicate entries on each credit report. If you had a credit card with ABC Bank and the balance was $1000 when it went to collections, you want to make sure that there's not a second entry from a debt collection agency or debt buyer. It may not even list ABC Bank. It may not even have the same account number. It might just list the same amount. You want to mark duplicate entries. They can hurt your credit, and you should not be penalized because of this. This is something that needs to be corrected.

o Look for debts that you truly don't recognize. This could be credit cards or revolving accounts that you

PARALEGAL'S GUIDE TO CREDIT REPAIR

never opened. It could even be medical bills. Medical fraud gets bigger and bigger each year.

o Look for accounts that are inaccurately reported. In the last chapter I mentioned how you should keep zero balance letters. This is why. If the company forgot to close out your account, it could be improperly recorded and hurt your credit.

o You'll also want to look for instances where debts are really, really old. We'll talk about the statute of limitations in this chapter, too.

Spreadsheet Set-up

As a paralegal that's worked in the bankruptcy industry, I swear by the use of a spreadsheet to keep up with creditors. You can set yours up in the way that works best for you. Mine has three tabs at the bottom. The first tab is the basic information related to the debt. I just call it 'Debt.' The second tab is for the disputing information. I call it 'Disputes.' The third tab is labeled as 'Communication.' It is where I log received information about debts.

With both the 'Disputes' and 'Communications' tab it is important that you log dates that you send letters, emails, or talk with someone on the phone. If you speak with someone on the phone, your notes need to include the phone number

PARALEGAL'S GUIDE TO CREDIT REPAIR

you called, the name of the person you spoke with, and the time (as well as notate what the conversation covered).

The 'Debt' tab is the first tab that you will set up. At the very least, it should list the company reporting, account number (even if it is just the last four digits reported), address of the company, the date that the debt was reported, the date the account was opened (if listed), the amount allegedly owed, and the statute of limitations. Here's a simple example:

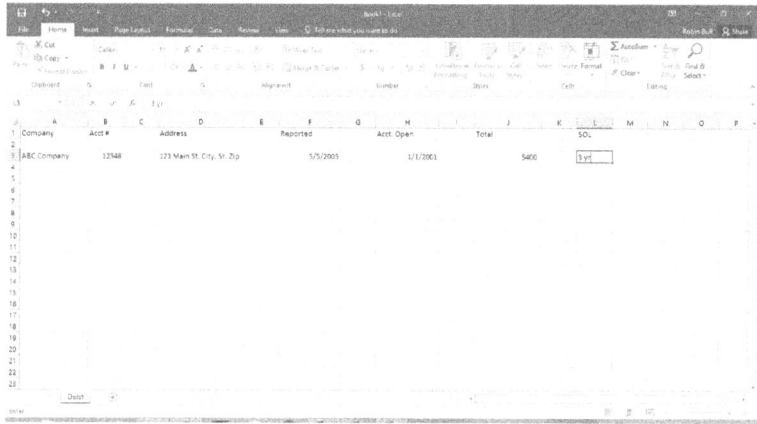

As you can see, there's nothing complicated about it. I skip columns and rows as I add information because it makes it easier for me to read when I refer to it later. You can set yours up however you like, but that's the basic info that you're going to need. You can also add a column to list which credit bureau

PARALEGAL'S GUIDE TO CREDIT REPAIR

it was reported to (Equifax, Transunion, etc.).

Now, here's an example 'Dispute' page. You'll notice that the column for 'Debt' doesn't repeat any information from the previous tab. I just refer to the cell location. One thing you should also do is either create a column for follow-up dates or just include it in your notes.

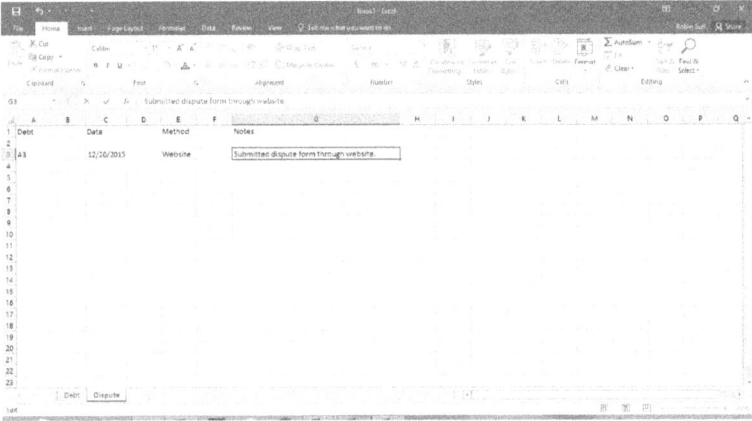

And now for the 'Communications' tab. As I stated, it is used simply to keep track of when I hear back on the disputes that I've submitted. I keep it simple. If you like fancier spreadsheets, knock yourself out. I prefer simplicity.

PARALEGAL'S GUIDE TO CREDIT REPAIR

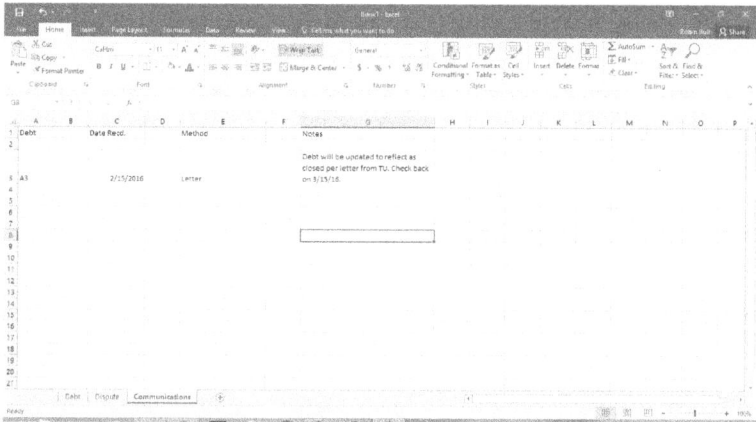

As you can see, I put in my notes the essence of the letter and when I should follow back up to ensure that the resolution suggested was implemented. Now, if you've been sent documentation or something else, you should note that.

Statute of Limitations

There were few things scarier to me as a paralegal and bankruptcy analyst than when I'd get a letter from the Trustee alleging that the statute of limitations had passed. Why? Because that meant that the client had no legal right to try and collect on the debt owed.

The statute of limitations for debt is different in each state. You're looking for the statute of limitations for your state.

PARALEGAL'S GUIDE TO CREDIT REPAIR

You must also know when the statute of limitations begins to run. It's also important that you understand what type of debt that you have because it does affect the statute of limitations (often abbreviated as SOL). There is a statute of limitations for written contracts, revolving accounts, and other forms of debt. You should do your due diligence to determine if you're debt qualifies as revolving or falls into another category. Again, I'm not an attorney and I won't toe the line of unauthorized practice of law to answer that for you. You can either consult with an attorney or do a thorough research job online to make that decision.

Finding the statute of limitations for your state is really, really easy. You can find it on close to any reputable public law site. My personal favorites are nolo.com and findlaw.com. You want to search "(your state) statute of limitations debt" or "(your state" statute of limitations collections." You could do the same search for credit cards, medical bills, or other debt. Again, remember that you need to understand the type of debt you have (written contract, revolving account, etc.) and when the statute of limitation begins. In many areas, it is often when the collections process begins. However, you should know that certain actions may retrigger the SOL. Unfortunately, listing those actions could get me into trouble since I'm not an attorney. So, please visit with an attorney or do some research on your own to make that determination. I advocate speaking with an attorney. Many are very, very

PARALEGAL'S GUIDE TO CREDIT REPAIR

helpful and there are great forums (such as avvo.com) that are reputable and where you may be able to get the answers that you need.

Fair Debt Collections Practices Act

No credit book would be complete without informing you about the Fair Debt Collections Practices Act (known as the FDCPA). This Act is available in plain language on the FTC's website. Just search "FDCPA for consumers."

Why do you need to know this Act if you're cleaning up your credit? Well, there could come a time where you find yourself on the phone with a debt collection agency. This Act tells you what they can and cannot say or do. For instance, they can call your neighbors, but only to try and get your contact information. They cannot call and threaten you with jail time or a criminal charge. They have to call during reasonable hours. They cannot call you at home or work after you tell them not to do it. They must provide proof of the debt if requested. They are not allowed to verbally abuse you.

If they violate the FDCPA, you need to document it. Of course, if you had the opportunity to record the violation, all the better. If not, you need to document the occurrence. Make sure that you get the person's name, phone number, and any other credentials. You can report violations of the Act to

PARALEGAL'S GUIDE TO CREDIT REPAIR

the FTC and to your state's attorney general. If it's particularly bad, you might speak with a civil law attorney to find out if you have a cause of action.

Proof of Debt

When you are disputing your debt, you will, in some instances, ask for proof of debt. As is stated by the FDCPA, creditors and collections agencies are required to provide it when asked. If they can't prove that you owe the debt, then they can't collect on it.

When I worked with banks and other corporate entities (as in before the debt was placed with a collections agency or sold to a debt buyer), I never worried when a Trustee would ask me to provide proof of debt. Those companies understand proof of debt and they keep copies of documents years. In this instance, they may use charge-off statements, credit card agreements that were signed, or the last three months of statements before the account was put into collections status. This documentation always listed the debtor, the amount owed, and the account number. The account number was usually redacted except for the last four digits.

Now, when I got a request from the Trustee because of a claim we filed on behalf of a debt buyer or collections agency, I just had to hold my breath and hope the client could provide

PARALEGAL'S GUIDE TO CREDIT REPAIR

something that would satisfy the Trustee.

3

Debt Buying Companies Have a Dirty Little Secret

It is fairly common that when an account goes into internal collections that it may be assigned a new account number. Now, when it's in collections with the company that originated the debt, it's typically fairly easy for that company to trace it back to the original account and come up with some sort of documentation that proves the debt exists. However, when that account is sold to a debt buyer, it gets harder to trace back those accounts to the original source to be able to provide documentation. That's because the company that buys the debt often changes the account number, and there's sometimes no trace of the original account number from the company. They may have an assignment letter (which they will most likely try to present as proof of debt), but they generally don't have access to signed agreements or anything else. Oh, and if they are unable to collect on it, they often sell it to

PARALEGAL'S GUIDE TO CREDIT REPAIR

someone else…which results in yet another change of account number. After a couple of years or so, it makes it increasingly hard for the debt buyer to present something that verifies that a debt is truly owed (because, again, they often cannot pull records back to the original account number or a signed agreement or application; sometimes they can't even provide invoices that were sent).

So, when I got those requests from the Trustee I would get into contact with the third party debt buyer to try and get documentation. If I didn't hear back from them within 14 business days, I withdrew their claim. It was better for the company that employed me if I withdrew the claim. It stopped the Trustee from objecting. It kept things peaceful in my world. The Trustees knew that if I was able to get the documentation from our clients that I would forward it. I didn't want to waste their time…or mine.

Alright, well, that's a nice story…what's that have to do with you?

In my experience as an analyst and someone who dealt with documentation, working on the third party debt accounts on your credit should be first on your list. What's a third party debt account? Well, it's going to be a name that you don't recognize. If you're unsure, take the name of the reporting company and look it up on the Internet. You'll find out fairly fast whether it's a third party debt buyer, a collection agency,

PARALEGAL'S GUIDE TO CREDIT REPAIR

or an actual company that thinks you owe them money. Often, you can identify them on your credit because it will list their name and then the entity that they are collecting for.

How to Dispute These Debts

I choose these debts first for one reason that you've hopefully caught on to by now…it's hard for them to verify the actual debt is owed. That's what makes these easy. You do have to make some decisions first, though.

You must decide if you want to dispute the legitimacy of the debt **or** if you want to mention that the statute of limitations has passed. Again, be careful with the statute of limitations. Certain actions can renew it. I urge you to ask an attorney or to do your own research to determine those actions. If you choose the statute of limitations, you need to know just how long that is for that particular type of debt. Refer to the last chapter to find out how you can do that.

Now, if you're only going to dispute the validity of the debt, you have two options.

1. Just go to the credit bureau website (for each of the three major credit bureaus) and file a dispute online. Since links change, I won't list the exact links. The easiest way to find them is to search online in this fashion: "Equifax dispute," "Transunion dispute," and

PARALEGAL'S GUIDE TO CREDIT REPAIR

"Experian dispute." You'll easily find the right page. Follow the instructions on each page. You will do this on all three credit bureau websites for each and every third party debt that you want to dispute. Generally, the creditor has 30 – 60 days to respond to the dispute. If they do not respond, it will be removed from your credit report.

2. You can send a certified letter to the third party debt buyer with return receipt requested disputing the validity of the debt and requesting that they send you proof of the debt in the form of a signed application or signed agreement between you and the original debtor. You should put language in the letter that states that your letter by no means is you taking responsibility for the debt. You found it on your credit report and you want it removed because you do not believe it is yours. Do not give them your phone number or you'll be called endlessly.

PARALEGAL'S GUIDE TO CREDIT REPAIR

4

Disputing Debts Is Easy

Disputing debts is easy. It doesn't take an expert. Again, if you elect to pay someone, please realize it is as a convenience service. If you follow the process below and use the letters that follow, you can dispute your own debts. Heck, the only reason why I charge for this material is because it covers the cost for the time I took away from my private clients to put this together. This is an informational product that you can use on your own. Disputing your debts is about one thing: being persistent if there really is no proof available that you owe something. It means that if the credit bureau comes back and says to you, "Well, the creditor says that you owe," that you ask for that documentation and remind the credit bureau that they can't just repeat what the creditor says. There must be proof that you owe the debt. You must be ready and willing to send letters that ask for verification and that push the issue of the credit bureau not having proof, but continuing to list something on your account. In this chapter, you're going to find letter templates that you can edit under a wide variety of circumstances. Also, you can find more letters

PARALEGAL'S GUIDE TO CREDIT REPAIR

listed on the FTC website.

I wanted you to start with the third party debt collectors and buyers because those are the easiest ones. Guess what? You use the same process for each and every debt on your credit that you want to dispute. So, again, you have two options:

1. Just go to the credit bureau website (for each of the three major credit bureaus) and file a dispute online. Since links change, I won't list the exact links. The easiest way to find them is to search online in this fashion: "Equifax dispute," "Transunion dispute," and "Experian dispute." You'll easily find the right page. Follow the instructions on each page. You will do this on all three credit bureau websites for each and every third party debt that you want to dispute. Generally, the creditor has 30 – 60 days to respond to the dispute. If they do not respond, it will be removed from your credit report.

2. You can send a certified letter to the company that says you owe them money with return receipt requested disputing the validity of the debt and requesting that they send you proof of the debt in the form of a signed application or signed. You should put language in the letter that states that your letter by no means is you taking responsibility for the debt. You found it on your credit report and you want it

PARALEGAL'S GUIDE TO CREDIT REPAIR

removed because you do not believe it is yours. Do not give them your phone number or you'll be called endlessly.

I prefer option #1 for just about everything. I'll tell you my personal reasoning behind that. I worked with companies all over the nation: banks, auto manufacturers, jewelry outlets, cell phone companies…I had a huge list of clients (and some banks were such a big pain in my butt when I requested documentation to protect their interests that I will never do personal business with them). My request was usually done by email or via spreadsheet that was then emailed. It had to go through their collections department and then usually on to the records department. They gathered up documentation and sent it back to me. Some clients were great and I could get what I needed within 24 hours. Some companies? I either never heard from them or I'd hear from them a month later. Disputing your debt through the credit bureau websites is much the same process, I imagine. You submit it to the credit bureau. Someone there has to look at it and attempt to contact the creditor. Then, the creditor has to hunt down the documentation. If they find it, they send it back. If they don't send it back in time or if they don't send anything at all, it can come off of your report. It's a time consuming process that many companies can't deal with.

Now, that's not to say that you'll be able to wipe everything

PARALEGAL'S GUIDE TO CREDIT REPAIR

from your credit. You may find some creditors do respond with debt verification documents. If that's the case, I urge you to move on to Chapter 5 to learn about settling your past due debts. First, though, here are some letter templates that you can use if you need them. Please double check all addresses **before you mail your letters.** Companies often change suites, addresses, or move to the use of PO Boxes. I cannot possibly keep up with each and every place now that this is no longer my main mode of employment.

Bounced Checks or Unpaid Debit Accounts

Your Name
123 A St.
City, State Zip

Reporting Agency
Customer Relations
Address
City, ST Zip

Dear Sir or Madam:

I was informed that there is negative information reported by NAME OF BANK included in the file COMPANY maintains under my Social Security Number. Upon ordering a copy of the report, I see an entry from this bank listing a "LIST TYPE OF DEBT SUCH AS BAD CHECK" in March 2007.

PARALEGAL'S GUIDE TO CREDIT REPAIR

I do not recall having a debit card from this bank during that time.

Please validate this information with BANK and provide me with copies of any documentation associated with this "debit card" bearing my signature. In the absence of any such documentation bearing my signature, I ask that this information be immediately deleted from the file you maintain under my Social Security Number.

Sincerely,

Signature
Name

Credit Bureau Verification Procedure Request

Sometimes, you get a notice that the credit bureau verified the debt. It is something that you have the right to know under the Fair Credit Reporting Act. It can be good to use during your dispute process.

Your Name
123 A St.
City, State Zip

PARALEGAL'S GUIDE TO CREDIT REPAIR

Credit Bureau Name
Address
City, State Zip

Date

Dear Sir or Madam:

This letter is a formal request for the description of the procedures used to determine the accuracy and completeness of the disputed information, including the business name, address, and telephone number of any furnisher of information contacted in connection with this reinvestigation, in compliance with the The Fair Credit Reporting Act, Section 611, part B, subsection (iii)

§ 611. Procedure in case of disputed accuracy [15 U.S.C. § 1681i]

(6)

(B) Contents. As part of, or in addition to, the notice under subparagraph (A), a consumer reporting agency shall provide to a consumer in writing before the expiration of the 5-day period referred to in subparagraph (A)

(i) a statement that the reinvestigation is completed;

PARALEGAL'S GUIDE TO CREDIT REPAIR

(ii) a consumer report that is based upon the consumer's file as that file is revised as a result of the reinvestigation;

(iii) a notice that, if requested by the consumer, a description of the procedure used to determine the accuracy and completeness of the information shall be provided to the consumer by the agency, including the business name and address of any furnisher of information contacted in connection with such information and the telephone number of such furnisher, if reasonably available;

I am disappointed that you have failed to maintain reasonable procedures to assure complete accuracy in the information you publish, and insist you comply with the law by providing the requested information within the 15 days allowed.

As a matter of convenience to you and to expedite my request, I am resubmitting my request to correct my credit report.

Name of Creditor/Agency, Account #_____

Your reasons for disputing this negative mark here, such as inaccurate account number, statute of limitations.

As already stated, the listed item is not accurate and is

PARALEGAL'S GUIDE TO CREDIT REPAIR

incomplete. This is a very serious error in reporting.

Sincerely,

Signature
Name
SSN

Debt Validation Letter

This simple letter simply requests that the creditor provide you with validation of the debt that they allege that you owe.

Your Name
123 A St.
City, State Zip

Creditor
Address
City, State Zip

Date

Re: Account # XXXX-XXXX

Dear Sir or Madam:

I just received your letter stating that you are collecting a debt

PARALEGAL'S GUIDE TO CREDIT REPAIR

on behalf of the <list company>. I have no idea what this debt is, and under my rights under the FDCPA, I request that you validate this debt.

Sincerely,

Signature
Name

Debt Validation Letter Using Statute of Limitations

This letter is something you can use if you plan to assert the statute of limitations. Remember what I told you earlier. I've seen some creditors do some tricky stuff with it and get away with it. And remember, certified mail with return receipt requested is your friend.

Your Name
123 A St.
City, State Zip

Creditor
Address
City, State Zip

Date

PARALEGAL'S GUIDE TO CREDIT REPAIR

Re: Account # XXXX-XXXX

Dear Sir or Madam:

I was recently made aware of a debt which is claimed to be in collection by your firm.

I'm sure you are aware of the provisions in the Fair Debt Collection Practices Act (FDCPA). I am requesting validation of this debt. I am requesting proof that I am the party you are asking to pay this debt, and there is some sort of contractual obligation which is binding. I request that your firm **not** contact me via telephone and restrict your contact with me to writing, and **only** when you can provide adequate validation of this alleged debt.

I'm sure you know, under FDCPA Section 809 (b), you are not allowed to pursue collection activity until the debt is validated. You should be made aware that in TWYLA BOATLEY, Plaintiff, vs. DIEM CORPORATION, No. CIV 03-0762 UNITED STATES DISTRICT COURT FOR THE DISTRICT OF ARIZONA, 2004, that the courts ruled that reporting a collection account on a credit report is considered collection activity.

I would like to point out that your agency has violated provisions of the FDCPA in the following respects:

15 USC 1692e(2)(A). falsely representing the legal status

PARALEGAL'S GUIDE TO CREDIT REPAIR

of the alleged debt. The statute of limitations on the original alleged debt, as reported on my credit report would have already have passed, therefore making the status uncollectable.

Non-compliance with this request could put your agency in serious legal trouble with the FTC and other state or federal agencies. Under the FCRA and the FDCPA, each violation is subject to a $1000 fine, payable to me.

Sincerely,

Signature
Name

Debt Validation Not Received By Collection Agency or Debt Buyer

Just because you don't get the validation doesn't mean that they'll automatically do what they're supposed to do. So, here's a nice little demand letter that you can use to assert your rights as outlined by the Fair Credit Reporting Act to the credit bureau.

Your Name
123 A St.
City, State Zip

PARALEGAL'S GUIDE TO CREDIT REPAIR

Creditor
Address
City, State Zip

Date

Re: Account # XXXX-XXXX

Dear Sir or Madam:

I am writing this letter to dispute the account referenced above. This account was previously disputed to you due to its inaccuracies on DATE. You responded come back to me and stated you were able to verify this debt. How is that possible?

Under the FDCPA, I have contacted the collection agency myself and have been unable to get verification that this is is my debt.

Enclosed, you will find copies of my requests to the collection agency asking for validation of this debt, and the return receipts showing that I sent these requested via certified mail with return receipt requested. This debt is not mine and I was given no evidence of my obligation to pay this debt to this collection agency.

The FCRA requires you to verify the validity of the item within 30 days. **If the validity cannot be verified, you are**

PARALEGAL'S GUIDE TO CREDIT REPAIR

obligated by law to remove the item. This is an unverified debt, and I urge you to remove this item before I am forced to pursue legal action.

In the event that you cannot verify the item pursuant to the FCRA, and you continue to list the disputed item on my credit report, I will find it necessary to consult an attorney to pursue actual damages and declaratory relief under the FCRA. According to this regulation, I may sue you in any qualified state or federal court, including small claims court.

While I prefer not to litigate, I will use the courts as needed to enforce my rights under the FCRA.

I look forward to an uneventful resolution of this matter.

Sincerely,

Signature
Name

Demanding the Credit Bureau Investigate and Not Just Agree With a Creditor

Sometimes, credit bureaus will just send you a response

PARALEGAL'S GUIDE TO CREDIT REPAIR

stating, "Well, the creditor said you owe them, so…." Fortunately for you, you have rights. Remember, you need to document everything in your spreadsheet. You also must be willing to follow up with any threats for legal action. That, of course, may need to be reviewed by an attorney to tell you whether or not you truly have a case.

Your Name
123 A St.
City, State Zip

Credit Bureau Name
Address
City, State Zip

Date

Dear Sir or Madam:

Recently, I submitted a request for investigation of an Acct Number# XXXX-XXX-XXXX, which you refused. I submitted enough information in my request for you to carry out a reasonable investigation of my dispute.

Had you taken the time to investigate properly, rather than use your e-Oscar system, you would have noticed INSERT REASON HERE (such as I am not sure that the account is even mine) – though your company claims to have "verified"

PARALEGAL'S GUIDE TO CREDIT REPAIR

this.

It is at this time that I will point out that in Cushman v. TransUnion, Stevenson v. TRW (Experian), and Richardson v. Fleet, Equifax, et al, that the courts ruled each and every time that the CRA couldn't just "parrot" information from the creditors and collection agencies. Credit agencies (you) must conduct an independent REASONABLE investigation to ensure the validity of the debt and the honesty and integrity of the creditor in question. Sending out a generic form through the e-Oscar system that does not even contain my reasons for the dispute *is not* reasonable.

If you do not initiate an investigation regarding my dispute, as is my right under the Fair Credit Reporting Act, I will have to take legal action to protect my credit rating and myself. As I'm sure you are aware, each violation of the Fair Credit Reporting Act allows damages of $1000 should this matter end up in court.

I look forward to an expedient resolution of this matter.

Sincerely,

Signature
Name

PARALEGAL'S GUIDE TO CREDIT REPAIR

SSN

Follow-up Letter

One reason why people pay others to do this for them is because it can be time consuming and it can require that you contact the credit bureau or creditor more than once. Here's a follow-up letter that you can modify for your personal use. You'll want to make sure that you list every time that you've attempted to contact them regarding this matter.

Your Name
123 A St.
City, State Zip

Credit Bureau Name
Address
City, State Zip

Date

RE: Dispute Letter of DATE YOU INITIALLY DISPUTED

Dear Sir or Madam:

This letter is formal notice that you failed to respond to my dispute letter of dated DATE HERE. I sent the initial letter

PARALEGAL'S GUIDE TO CREDIT REPAIR

registered mail (OR I SUBMITTED MY DISPUTE ONLINE) and have enclosed a copy of the return receipt that was signed.

As you are well aware, federal law requires you to respond within 30 days. It has now been over that period since your receipt of my letter. As you are no doubt are aware, failure to comply with federal regulations by credit reporting agencies is a serious violation of the Fair Credit Reporting Act, and may be investigated by the FTC. Please be aware that I am maintaining detailed records of all my correspondence with you.

I am aware that you may have misplaced my request or have failed to respond because of an oversight due to the high volume of the requests you receive. If this is the case, I'm sure you'll want to handle this matter as soon as possible. For this purpose, I have included a copy of my original request, the dated receipt of your reception of the original letter, and a copy of the proof verifying the inaccuracy of the credit item you have mistakenly placed on my records.

The following information needs to be verified and deleted from my credit report as soon as possible:

CREDITOR, acct. XXXX-XXXX-XXXX-XXXX

Sincerely,

PARALEGAL'S GUIDE TO CREDIT REPAIR

Signature
Name
SSN

Purpose of Inquiry Letter

When you're reviewing your credit, you'll notice that there are companies that have made an inquiry about your credit. Too many requests to view your credit file can have a negative impact on your credit. If you see something that you don't recognize, you need to find out why that particular entity is looking to get a copy of your credit file. Make sure that you send this letter certified with a return receipt requested.

Your Name
123 A St.
City, State Zip

Entity
Address
City, State Zip

Date

PARALEGAL'S GUIDE TO CREDIT REPAIR

Dear Sir or Madam:

As per my Equifax/Transunion/Experian credit report, your company obtained my credit file on _____.

I don't recall applying for credit or employment with your company.

From the FCRA § 616. Civil liability for willful oncompliance [15 U.S.C. § 1681n]

"(b) Civil liability for knowing noncompliance. Any person who obtains a consumer report from a consumer reporting agency under false pretenses or knowingly without a permissible purpose shall be liable to the consumer reporting agency for actual damages sustained by the consumer reporting agency or $1,000, whichever is greater."

From the 1998 FTC opinion letter Greenblatt at http://www.ftc.gov/os/statutes/fcra/greenblt.htm:

"Any person who procures a consumer report under false pretenses, or knowingly without a permissible purpose, is liable for $1000 or actual damages (whichever is greater) to both the consumer and to the consumer reporting agency from which the report is procured."

PARALEGAL'S GUIDE TO CREDIT REPAIR

Please explain your permissible purpose for your obtaining my credit file. Please note that non-permissible inquiries to credit are punishable by fine.

Sincerely,

Signature
Name

Reinserted Items

Sometimes, you may notice that items are removed and then added back to your credit report. This is why it is important that you pay attention to your credit file. If this happens to you, you can modify this letter and send it via certified mail with a return receipt requested.

Your Name
123 A St.
City, State Zip

Credit Bureau
Address
City, State Zip

Date

Re: Account: XXXX-XXXX-XXX

PARALEGAL'S GUIDE TO CREDIT REPAIR

SSN: XXXX (last four)
DOB: XX/XX/XXXX

Dear Sir or Madam:

I disputed the above referenced account on DATE. The credit report dated DATE and your report to me shows that these items was deleted from my credit file. I recently noticed that these items were reinserted on my credit report.

In accordance with the requirements of the FCRA as shown below, I am hereby requesting your complete compliance with any and all of the provisions:

FCRA § 611, Procedure in case of disputed accuracy [15 U.S.C. § 1681i]

Requirements relating to reinsertion of previously deleted material.

Certification of accuracy of information. If any information is deleted from a consumer's file pursuant to subparagraph (A), the information may not reinserted in the file by the consumer reporting agency unless the person who furnishes the information certifies the information is complete and accurate.

PARALEGAL'S GUIDE TO CREDIT REPAIR

If any information that has been deleted from a consumer's file pursuant to subparagraph (A) is reinserted in the file, the consumer reporting agency shall notify the consumer of the reinsertion in writing not later than 5 business days after the reinsertion or, if authorized by the consumer for that purpose, by any other means available to the agency. Additional information. As part of, or in addition to, the notice under clause (ii), a consumer reporting agency shall provide to a consumer in writing no later than 5 business days after the reinsertion date.

(I) a statement that the disputed information has been reinserted;

(II) the business name and address of any furnisher of information contacted and the telephone number of such furnisher, if reasonably available, or of any furnisher of information that contacted the consumer reporting agency, in connection with the reinsertion of such information; and

(III) a notice that the consumer has the right to add a statement to the consumer's file disputing the accuracy or completeness of the disputed information.

I received no such notification as required. This is a serious violation of the FCRA, and I reserve the right to pursue legal action. Your agency may avoid such action by immediately

PARALEGAL'S GUIDE TO CREDIT REPAIR

deleting this listing from my credit report.

Sincerely,

Signature
Name

Requesting Removal of Inaccurate Information Via Letter

I far prefer the digital process of removing inaccuracies, but sometimes letters get the job done. They're easy to track as long as you carefully document it and send it via certified mail with return receipt requested (and make copies of each letter that you send out). If you have proof that a debt does not belong to you or that you've paid something off in full, you should send a copy of it with your letter.

Your Name
123 A St.
City, State Zip

Credit Bureau
Address
City, State Zip

PARALEGAL'S GUIDE TO CREDIT REPAIR

Date

SSN:
DOB:

Dear Sir or Madam:

This letter is a formal complaint and dispute against the inaccurate credit information on my credit report.

I am very disappointed that you included the information noted below in my credit profile due to its damaging effects on my credit. As you no doubt are aware, credit reporting laws ensure that bureaus report only accurate credit information. No doubt the inclusion of this inaccurate information is a mistake either on your or the creditor's part. Because of the mistakes on my credit report, I have been wrongfully denied credit recently for LIST RECNT DENIAL, which was highly embarrassing and negatively impacted my lifestyle.

With the proof I'm attaching to this letter, I'm sure you'll agree that the inaccurate information is harmful to me and needs to be immediately removed.

The following information should be verified and deleted from the report as soon as possible:

PARALEGAL'S GUIDE TO CREDIT REPAIR

CREDITOR, Acct. # XXXX-XXX-XXXX-XXXX

Sincerely,

Signature
Name

Other Instances Where You May Need a Letter

Hopefully, you don't find yourself in a position where you have to use too many of those demand letters. In addition to working as a bankruptcy analyst and paralegal, I've helped people fix their credit. More often than not, it doesn't take but a couple of letters back and forth to get things resolved. Generally, the hard part is waiting. They have 30 days to respond, but if you're going back in forth, it can get long (hence my earlier comments about 30 – 90 days).

Now, there may be other instances where you are in need of a letter. What I provided you with are the common letters that I've used. The good news is that this is the information age. You can find letter examples all over the Internet. The FTC consumer site is a great place to start. They have sample letters, too.

PARALEGAL'S GUIDE TO CREDIT REPAIR

You may need a letter to stop debt collectors from calling you. Remember to send all letters as certified with a return receipt requested. I know it's expensive, but that's the ONLY way that you'll know for sure that they received your letter.

You may also need a letter if you agree to settle. We'll talk a little bit about settlement in the next chapter, but I want to say one thing about that right now: get everything in writing and do not give them access to your bank account. This is another instance where letters are your friend.

With any letter you send, always make copies. Copy more than the letter. Copy everything that you send in the letter (if you include any documentation). Do not ever send your original documentation. When you prepare your certified mail form with return receipt, make sure that when you get it back (signed from the other party) that you staple it to the copies that you made. Document, document, document…just in case you really do decide to talk to an attorney, the FTC, or the attorney general of your state about your legal options.

I'd like to say one other thing about debt that I hope that anyone who reads this already knows: if there is something that you truly don't recognize (or multiple things) please follow the appropriate guidelines for reporting suspected identity theft. I don't care if your 18 or 81, it can happen to you. I know some young people that had incorrect listings on their credit because of their parents using their personal info.

PARALEGAL'S GUIDE TO CREDIT REPAIR

I know it's family, but it is still identity theft. If you're an adult, do not use your child's information. Cleaning up credit isn't any fun particularly when you did nothing to incur a debt to begin with.

I am not an identity theft expert. Please contact the authorities and consult the FTC and the credit bureaus for more information about how you can clean up your credit in the instance of identity theft.

5

What You Need to Know About Debt Settlement

So, once you have all of the inaccuracies taken care of, it's time to take care of the debt that you actually owe. I recommend following Dave Ramsey's get out of debt plan (he offers the basics online for free) which, after saving up a small emergency fund, means that you list your debts from smallest to largest and you start by paying off your smallest debt. Now, it could be that it's not worth settling…and just paying it in full. Either way, what I'm about to say next is very important:

Do not give creditors access to your bank account. Take the money that you plan to put toward that debt and place it on a prepaid debit card that is NOT LINKED to your primary bank account. Because if you give them your bank info even for a one time draft, they will drain your account. Don't put yourself in that situation. Finally, you call them and tell them that you're going to pay and you get the pay off amount in writing. Once you pay it, keep your proof of payment and

PARALEGAL'S GUIDE TO CREDIT REPAIR

then call and get a zero balance statement. Keep these things…because debt collectors are liars. They'll try to keep calling you to get you to pay more. They'll say things like you owe more than you did. Send them a copy of your zero balance statement and tell them to get lost.

Now, here's what you need to know about settling. Most places sell their debt for pennies on the dollar to other entities. Once you've ascertained who is the legal owner of the debt, start haggling with them. This is probably going to take more than one call. They'll tell you several times they can't accept any less than what you owe. That's just not true. Just hang up on them and call back later and do it again. Eventually, you'll get someone who will take a settlement amount. When they agree, have them send you the settlement agreement in writing. Do not pay until you get that letter. This is your proof that they have agreed to a settlement with you. Then, as I said in the last paragraph you need to use a prepaid debit card OR you can use a money order or a cashier's check. If you give those people access to your bank account, you will regret it. Once you have your letter and you send them the entire payment, you need to get proof that it was paid. When you initially settle with them, talk to them about updating your credit report to paid and closed. This can help your credit score when compared to it saying delinquent or charged off.

That's it. That's everything that you need to know in order to

PARALEGAL'S GUIDE TO CREDIT REPAIR

fix your own credit. It doesn't take an expert. It doesn't take someone like me. You just need the time and the ability to keep with it. Remember, keep good documentation of your contact with the credit bureaus and the creditors. Then, once you get out of debt, do your best to stay out.

PARALEGAL'S GUIDE TO CREDIT REPAIR

Stay in touch with the author via:

Twitter: http://twitter.com/#!/@TheRobinBull
Facebook: http://www.facebook.com/TheRobinBull

Please post a review at Amazon, and let your friends know about this book. Caring really is sharing!

www.ingramcontent.com/pod-product-compliance
Lightning Source LLC
Chambersburg PA
CBHW061448180526
45170CB00004B/1613